back to me

carly jean puch

To every single person who helped pull me through my darkness,
thank you will never be enough.

contents

words written across my body

. . .

EASILY SEEN but not easily understood.

They itch.

I scratched.

It only makes them burn brighter.

They burn.

I cool them.

It only makes them louder.

But then I listen.

They don't want to be read.

They want to be heard.

To be read risks misunderstanding.

To be heard assures the message is conveyed.

When listened to, the words don't hurt.

They don't itch; they tickle.

They don't burn; they feel like the wind from forgotten places blowing into consciousness.

They are still easily seen but even more easily understood.

what was different about you

. . .

I HAVE STORIES.

I'm a woman, after all.

When I told you stories of brokenness, you didn't try to fix them.

You didn't try to mend them with threads of "I'm sorry" or wrap me in fragile tape.

No, you were different.

You showed me your rips and tears and picked up my pieces in a gesture of understanding.

I followed suit and carefully wrapped yours in my softest sweater of validation and cotton.

I had gotten it wrong in the past, looking for a fix when I just needed a safe place for my pieces.

You've become the treasure chest on the island I swam to.

The land I had punished myself for being too much to handle for the rest of the world.

But you are different.

You turned my pieces into gold.

trauma

. . .

THE TRAUMA TAKES hold in the deepest darkest parts of us.

It clings to our memories and makes our bodies ache with feelings.

It crawls out in times of joy to try and steal the light.

In the moments that feel unrelated but somehow, that's when it happens.

Shake it loose; make it move through you.

At some point, it becomes impossible not to let it go; throw it out of your body.

Take control of it back into your hands.

The healing spiral is a well-worn path by the warriors who came before us.

Sometimes you may be unsure if you're walking toward home or back into the terror because the path is a circle.

North can be rugged.

But then you look down and see your feet still moving even though your head made you think you had stopped.

Feel the pain of those on this path before me; let it move you forward.

i didn't understand

. . .

I DIDN'T UNDERSTAND how you didn't love yourself.
 I didn't understand that you couldn't see it.
 I see rainbows and light and sparkles.
 How are you not blinded by it?
 I'm sorry you don't see it. I'm sorrier you don't feel it.
 I hope you will. I want to see the moment you do.
 That will be a connection felt by the world.

do you love me?

. . .

WHEN ASKING someone if they love you, you're avoiding answering the question yourself.

Can our senses stop recognizing what home is?

The smell of you no longer feels comforting, but like a stranger, I've known forever.

Remember loving how someone smells?

Do you still love me?

The sense was so powerful it could stop our minds from racing, or the sight of each other's bodies filled us with instant comfort, the sound of groggy morning voices brought peace in knowing each other was there.

Maybe we just shut down our senses, perhaps they shut down, and we didn't even know. I know it's not too late to breathe in and reminisce.

Or feast my eyes over the shape of your soul in my memories.

Or hear you whisper that you love me.

Do you love me?

It comes back if allowed.

I stopped allowing it.

depression

. . .

THE FIRST TIME my therapist mentioned depression, I was furious.

I was having a hard time - I was NOT depressed.

I had othered depressed people so far from myself that my nostrils flared at the mention.

Heat rising in my chest, I riddled her with questions. I was hoping to prove that she was wrong.

It ebbs and flows with the changing of the tides.

It's more than sadness. Sadness ends.

When you're depressed, you're worried it won't.

It feels like the tiniest task will break you inside.

Some of us like to think of ourselves as high-functioning depressed.

The facade is high functioning, but the reality is depression.

You are not the feeling of hopelessness that feels all-consuming.

You are so many other things. That is just one part.

It's a piece of the complete puzzle that is you.

Honor all the pieces.

two things are true

. . .

IT WAS EASIER to write about what pissed me off.

Easier to fuel the fire of mistrust.

We always want to act as we know.

We pretend that we were smart enough to see all the breadcrumbs left behind on the path to destruction.

It was harder to admit I had no idea.

That denial was the only substance I was sipping on.

But the best part?

Admitting there was pure joy.

Admitting there was love.

We think love prevents terror.

I've decided not to resent the love that taught me so much.

Thanks for the memories.

strength

. . .

"YOU'LL BE OK; you're strong. I don't have to worry about you."

And there was the problem, a problem... one of many purposefully avoided problems.

Just because I'm strong doesn't mean I don't want you to care.

I desperately wanted to be cared for.

I was tired of faking flattery so that people could walk away from me without me crumbling.

You'll be ok. You're strong.

Stuck in the glue of binary thinking – people are or aren't.

They're here or there but never allowed to be everywhere.

To be strong and self-assured while also desiring the support and strength of the energetic match.

You'll be ok. You're strong.

I know I'm strong. I'm still here, aren't I?

I want to be complimented for my strength and celebrated for my vulnerability.

I want to be complimented for my vulnerability and celebrated for my strength.

I am both.

grief

. . .

I THOUGHT grief was only for physical deaths.

So, when he left, I didn't have the tools.

Only the broken parts are in a hastily packed box.

He wasn't gone, but he was.

After stumbling through weeks of sadness, I started to grieve.

I grieved until the sound of his name didn't bring tears to my eyes

and until the old photos were put away for another time.

Then I learned the truth.

And the grieving started again.

But now I was in familiar terrain.

I didn't want him to have that much power over me still.

And he doesn't.

Because after grief comes rebirth,

a rearranging of what I know to be true.

And not so scared of suffering.

Every ego death and unlearned pattern must be grieved to be honored.

Because, oddly, it's what brings you home.

silver lining

. . .

SOMETIMES SILVER LININGS ARE BULLSHIT.

Can you learn from tragic, life-altering experiences?

Of course.

But don't tell me to look for silver linings when I'm still seeing red.

Don't shove "everything happens for a reason" down my throat so often I wonder if I enjoy the taste.

It's hard to trust the process when you're in the middle.

The sticky, unsure, messy time where tears and snot flow from your body at random.

When crying yourself to sleep is a part of your daily routine.

I didn't know what it was like to fall asleep without a tear-soaked pillowcase.

Don't tell someone to trust the process when they're here.

You never realize you feel better right away.

Pieces come back together until, one day, you look in the mirror and recognize yourself.

The relief washes over you as you exhale and welcome yourself home.

I'll tell you when my lining is silver and gold again.

the moon

. . .

RELIGION NEVER FELT right to me, like an itchy wool jacket I couldn't wait to get out of.

What does feel right is pausing in gratitude every time I see the moon.

Smiling at its presence like a comforting matriarch's smile at the people.

A constant reminder of the movement and ever-changing sky.

Something to count on in a world that feels like too much — a world that suffocates you until you can't breathe.

I look to the moon.

i knew

. . .

I OFTEN KNOW what needs to be done.

I knew it was over.

I knew when the sand had stopped running, and the tide had stopped turning.

When saltwater and freshwater collide, it's called brackish water.

This in-between space becomes its ecosystem, supporting a particular array of plants and animals.

I thought brackish water was gross at one time – this in-between place that you wouldn't want to stay in – you wanted to be on either side of it.

But it's supposed to be there.

It supports you as you move from one place in the water to the next.

Life is full of salty water.

You might as well swim.

forgive

. . .

MY ABILITY TO forgive does not make me weak.

The misconception that you must hold on to the bitterness of past wrongs is toxic.

Resentment is poison to your higher self.

It feeds the ego and keeps you on the line.

That other person doesn't give two shits about this situation you keep yourself tied to.

Get untangled from the string.

regret

. . .

I'VE DECIDED to stop living in regret.

In too many moments, I become rooted in what-ifs with no action.

What ifs are the questions that keep you up when the stars are out.

The questions that steal from your ability to be present.

The questions that cause your anxiety to spike and your foundation to shake.

Regret isn't the answer.

Not even if you were a shitty person.

Regret won't erase that moment.

Action will.

space

. . .

SPACE IS one of those things we can't make up our minds about.

We want space from people, places, obligations, and life - we feel suffocated.

Then we get to space, and there's too much air.

We don't know how to breathe in freshness when our lungs have learned to survive pollution.

The thing about living in tiny places is that space is limited.

You don't have a choice.

But it's not space we're indifferent to.

It's us.

It's spending time with our thoughts that make us crave change.

But no matter what, we end up back with ourselves.

Better to love yourself now.

You are your only true ride-or-die.

Time to ride.

spiral

. . .

HEALING IS like journeying on a spiral despite being discussed as a linear path, easy as crossing the street.

But the directions are far less clear.

It is winding and stumbling.

It's thinking you've completed the task at hand only to be slapped by a memory, a sound, a touch.

Once I followed the spiral like Alice down the rabbit hole, it all got easier.

Some paths make you smaller.

Some paths make you larger.

None of them lead to the answer.

All of them do.

You can decide.

You pick up advice along the way.

Some are sage, and some are shit.

What do you choose?

the magic

. . .

I THINK we're born believing in magic.

The world hardens us. A seed of doubt is planted one day, and it grows - sometimes more quickly, but, oh, do we nourish it.

Our hearts are cold even when we remember it's too good to be true.

I thought I was special, that my belief in magic was fully intact. I thought I had skated through adolescence without it wasting away.

Then he broke my heart.

When it came down to it, I was just as cold as him.

What a messy awakening.

Oh, how confident break when emotions are at stake.

I saw the world for what others must have seen while I stayed steeped in my privilege and naivete - pain and misery steady as the sunrise.

But I survived. Even in the darkness, when the patience to feel better had dwindled to crumbs - I still survived.

And so did you. So are you. So will you.

I guess magic is real.

ego death

. . .

THE DEATH of the ego is not a death that needs mourning.
It needs a big parade, an honoring, a celebration.
You met that part of you and realized you didn't need it anymore.
Rejoice.
Don't wear black.

freedom

. . .

YOU DON'T KNOW what you've lost until you get it back.

At least, that's how it was with my freedom.

We trick ourselves into believing we're in control of situations even when we're not.

It soothes the pain of knowing control is the ultimate illusion.

I marched in D.C.

I own a pink pussy hat.

I'm a feminist, damn it.

I can't lose control in a relationship with a MAN.

But I did.

Every day my inner knowing screamed at me to walk away.

But my ego was attached to the vision without addressing the shadows.

That muddiness led to staying.

Staying when I knew it was over. I stayed in love with the idea of love.

I was determined to avoid rejection.

My freedom is back. I do all the things I want to do without the fear of silent rejection.

i'm not surprised

. . .

I WONDER what you think of me now.

Would you be surprised?

That I did all the things, we said we would do?

I'm not. I always knew I could.

Somebody had to.

Well, that's what I thought at first.

It turns out I wasn't doing it because I had to.

But because I had been me the entire time.

The moon may have waxed and waned, and with it, challenge aplenty.

But I was still me.

Can you say the same?

the best part

. . .

THE BEST PART - nobody knows what they're doing.

Something is comforting in knowing we're all just struggling to figure out how to navigate this place.

It connects us all – our shared humanity, confusion, and search for love and understanding.

Sometimes we walk down the right path and run from it. But it's not about getting caught up in not knowing what you're doing; it's how you handle the pivot.

when i

. . .

I LIVE BETTER when I slow down to process, think, and not think.

There are so many signs of my manifestations.

Instantly desires arrive if it's for the highest good.

Be patient. It's already here.

Signs start flooding in when I am consistent in my beliefs and practices.

Precisely, it's aligning as it should.

My everyday language matters.

I don't need to take in the fears and concerns of others.

I know the truth from my heart.

It's all mine.

Don't get stuck asking. The Universe heard you – allow goodness.

blind

. . .

I DON'T WANT my love to be blind anymore.

My eyes are open, and I want to see it all.

When love is blind, you block the messy parts, but if the dirty details are missing, is it love?

When I made being wrong an exciting moment to learn instead of a devastating ego blow, my life got easier. "I'm wrong? Then I get to learn."

"Just so you know, this is what love feels like," she said as she held him tight for as many moments as his heart could handle.

I wonder if he felt it.

But I know it was there. It's not my job to see if he felt it. It's only my job to give it.

Sometimes you give love and don't get to feel its effects for minutes, hours, days - decades.

But if you give without having to know, it does come back.

Have patience, my loves.

present stealers

. . .

IT WAS when I was eating pizza one day.

I couldn't bring myself to order our favorite.

I was harkening back to when we walked through fields, holding hands and imagining the future.

Do you remember that moment when we stood on the edge of a cliff?

I made you stop and close your eyes to see if you saw what I saw. You said you did.

I believed you.

But maybe you did. Maybe *us* was *ours*, and that was that.

We stopped doing that.

I stopped doing that.

You close your eyes, breathe deeply, and feel grateful.

We robbed our lives of the present to live in the past.

I preferred to ruminate in the past.

The pizza was good. It's my new favorite.

big world

. . .

THE WORLD IS MORE significant than me – despite me being the only one I see.

But looking deeper, changing the focus to the backdrop of my existence reveals my small space in it all.

But I remember that removing myself makes it fall – we need all the tiny spaces that make up the prominent places - so our spirits have room to wander.

We were swimming through waves of the ego to a place that, once we go, seems permanent.

But nothing stays. It floats away to move you to the next perfect moment.

The Universe knows what she's doing.

You will, too, if you listen.

you need healing too

. . .

WHEN YOU'RE someone who fancies themselves as self-aware as this little Pisces does, it's easy to trick yourself into thinking you're "ok."

It's easy-- preferred, really -- to focus on the people around you and try to improve their lives while secretly hoping it will fix you too.

All the while letting yourself believe you're not that bad.

You, of all people, would know!

But *you're* not ok. And that's ok.

You should deal with that first.

Helping others from an unhealed place can do damage you're not even aware of until the explosion.

The helpers need help.

The caregivers need care given back.

But you must accept it.

Allow the love and guidance that feels good to lift you back up to the heavenly state you deserve to embody.

Manifesting your desires requires allowing, but it also means intentional action. You won't always need to meet half-way, but some of the way.

Start. Heal. Become.

back to me

. . .

I WAS ashamed of continuing to hold on to love, of having faith it will all be ok.

Isn't it stronger to remain jaded?

That's what I thought.

That's all I knew.

It turns out you're stronger when you speak it out loud.

It turns out that feeling the softness is harder.

It turns out it's worth it.

It got me here.

Back to me.

I'll hold this love forever.

It led me to me.

about the author

Carly Jean Puch is a meditation enthusiast who sits quietly every morning and a lover of blasting 90's hip-hop at total volume. She's a gym rat and a yoga instructor. She is both learner and a teacher. We are all many things. Together we can make them all work. Carly loves to share all the things she's learning along the way. Learning how to be your most conscious self but being honest about how damn hard and messy it can be along the way lets you speak our truth. It allows us to use our voices for the causes that matter to us.

Carly hosts the Consciously Clueless podcast and works as a Conscious Living Coach. On the podcast and in her coaching she incorporates mindfulness, sustainability, and plants to help people change their personal lives so they can help change the world. Carly also teaches yoga and is currently teaches to both adults and kids grades 1st-8th grades. Carly works construction part-time and is excited to keep working on her school bus turned tiny home on wheels!

9798988125105